To my goddaughter, Sophia Isabella Fox,
and my godson, Michael Alexander Munro

Book design by Kristine Brogno.
Jacket design by Mary Beth Fiorentino.
Typeset in Kosmik-Plain Three.
The illustrations in this book were rendered in India ink and colored inks.
Manufactured in Hong Kong.

Library of Congress Cataloging-in-Publication Data available.

Distributed in Canada by Raincoast Books
9050 Shaughnessy Street, Vancouver, British Columbia V6P 6E5

10 9 8 7 6 5 4 3 2 1

Chronicle Books LLC
85 Second Street, San Francisco, California 94105

www.chroniclekids.com

AMAZEMENT PARK

ROXIE MUNRO

chronicle books · san francisco

PARK RULES

Your fun starts here! Each ride or attraction is a maze and connects to the one on the next page.

When you get to the Minotaur Maze at the end, turn around and make your way back on a different path.

There are two ways to go through Amazement Park.

You can take the red Toot-Toot Train by all the rides and attractions, or you can take the maze journey through the rides and attractions (this way is harder but fun!).

On your way, look for the man with three balloons in each maze.

Find Mrs. McCourt and her school class in all the mazes.

Check out the ice-cream stands—there's one in each maze.

What other games can you create and play with this book?

Have fun!

The answers begin on page 32.

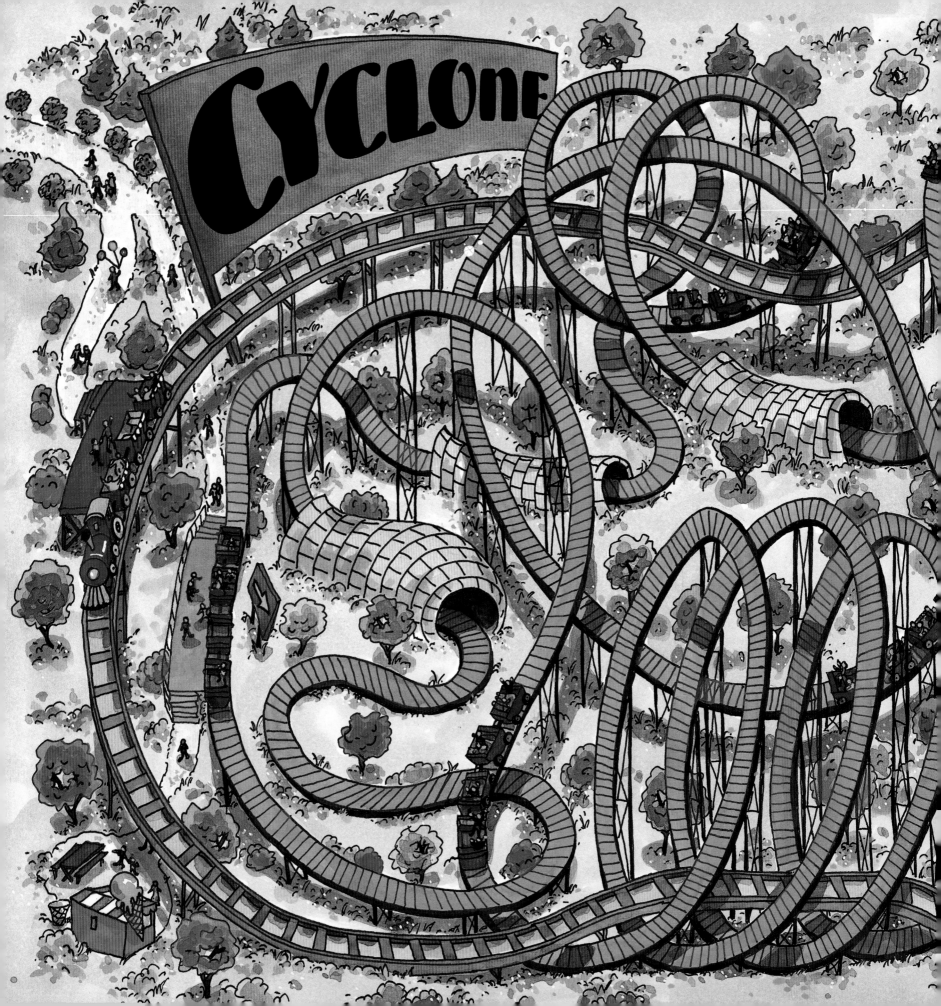

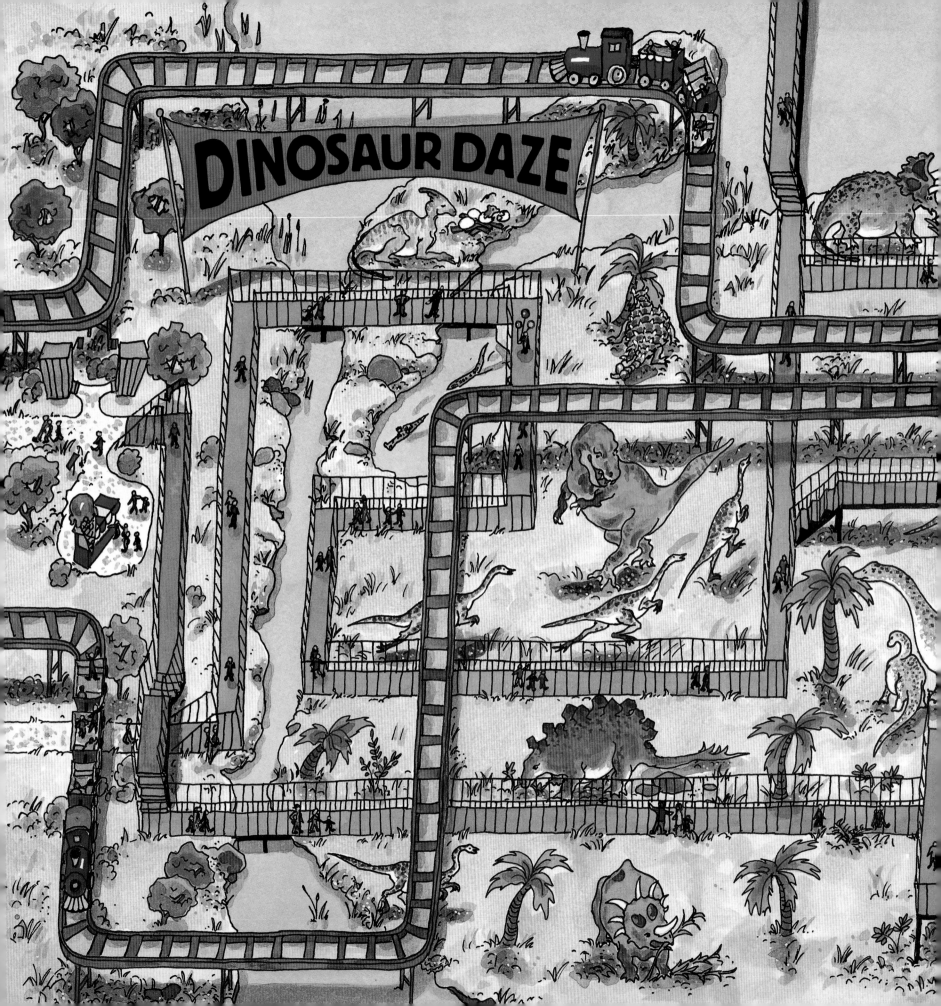

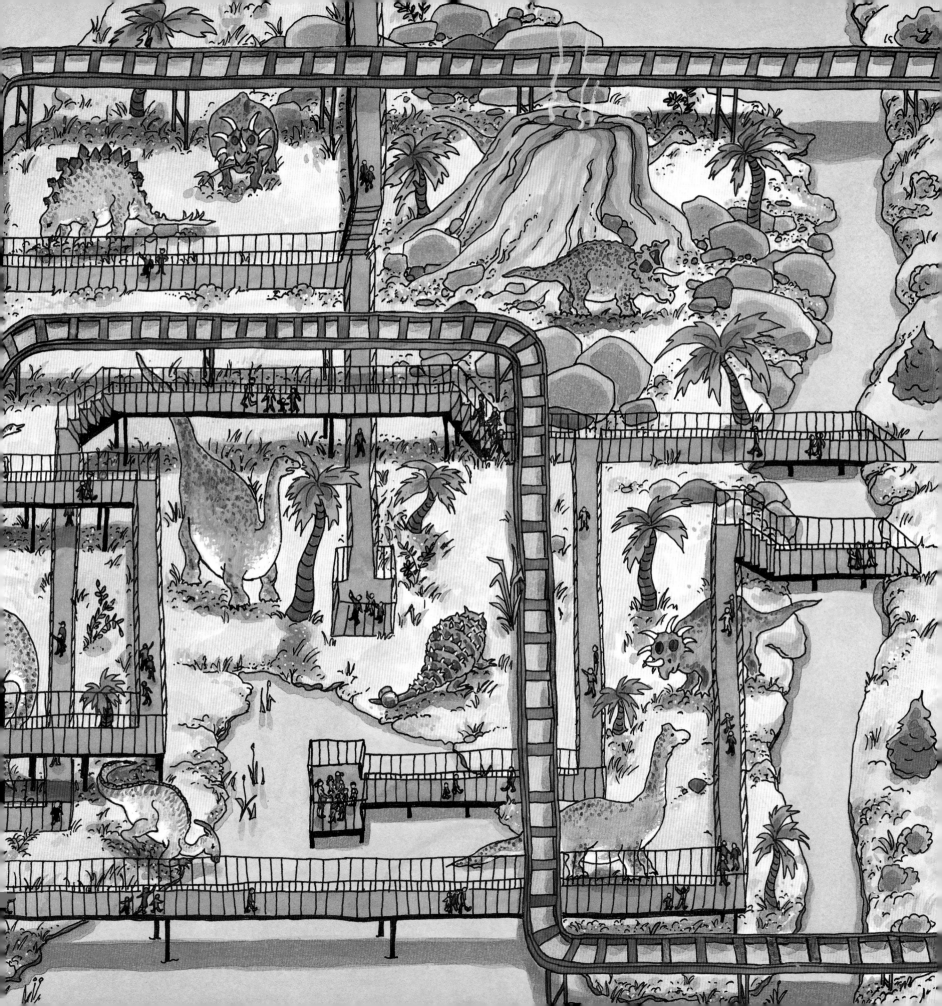

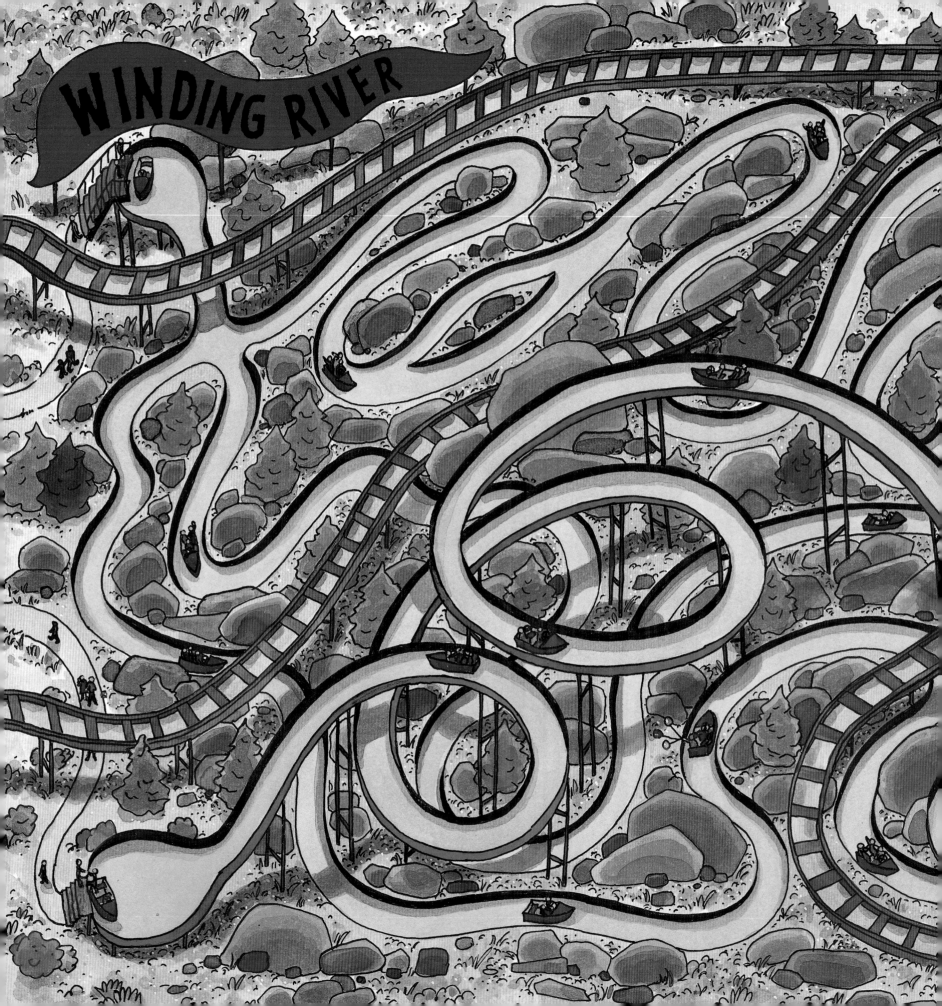

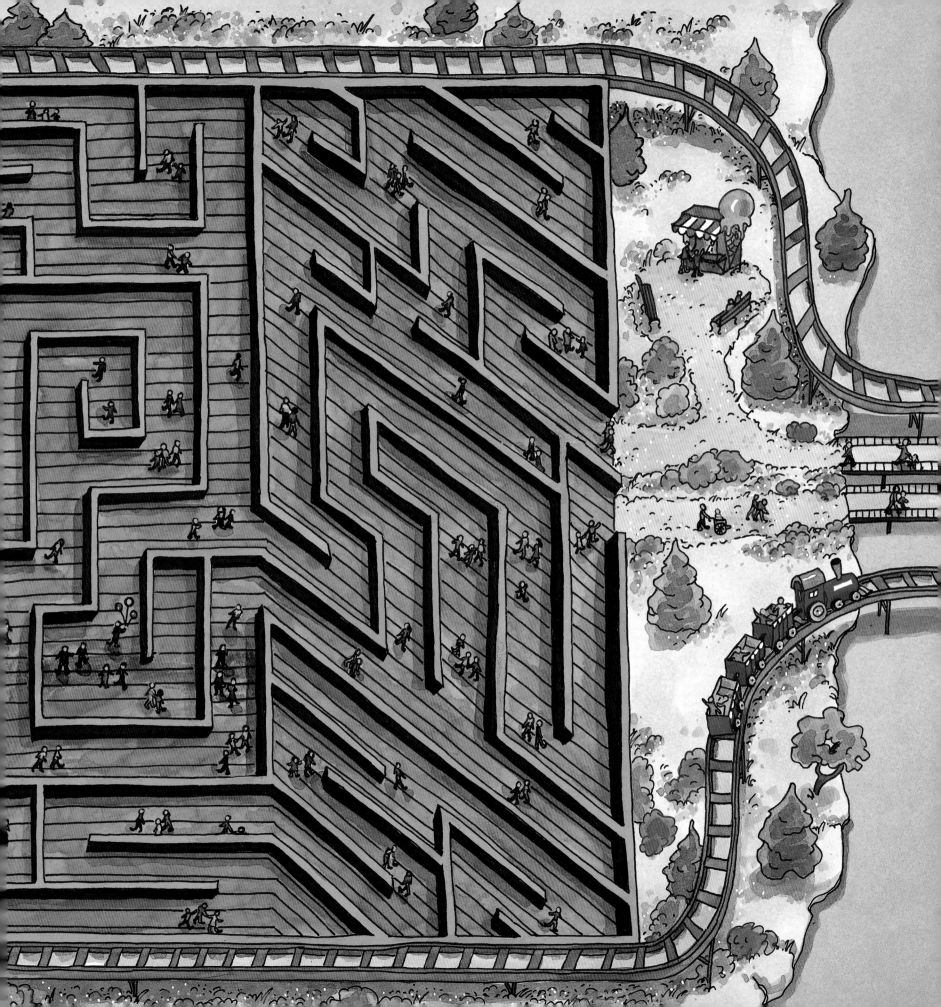

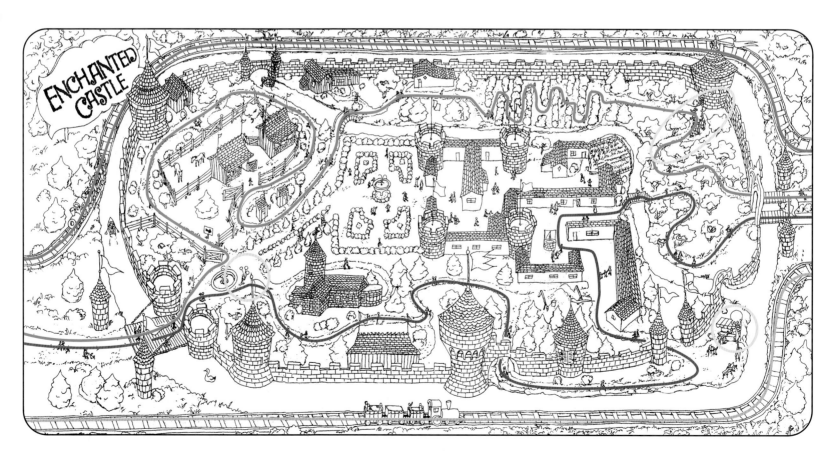

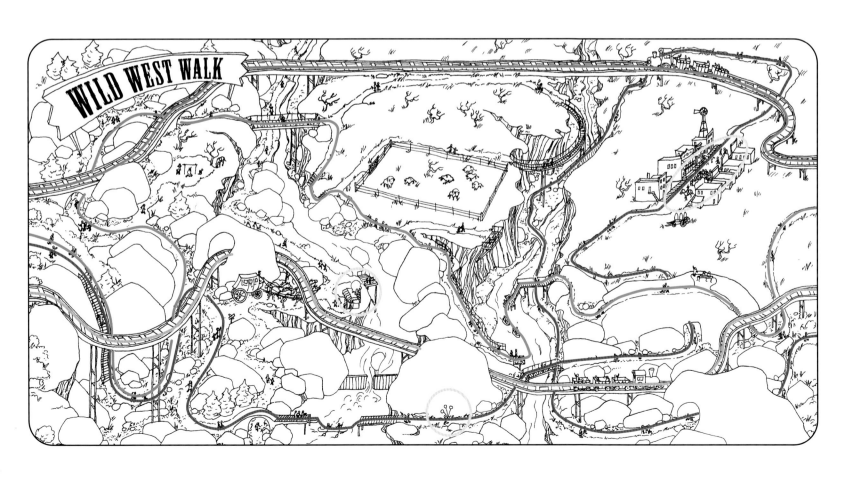

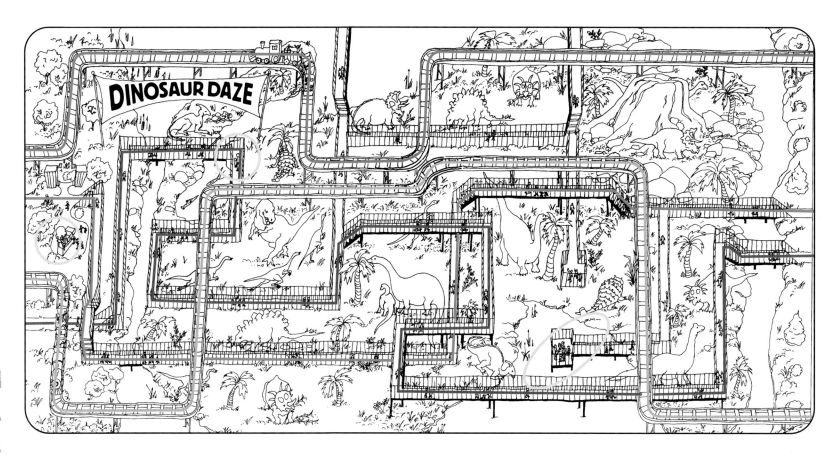

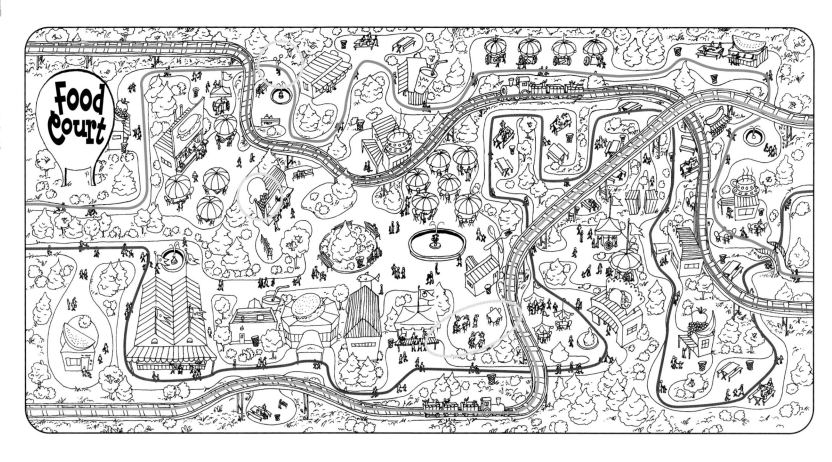

WINDING RIVER

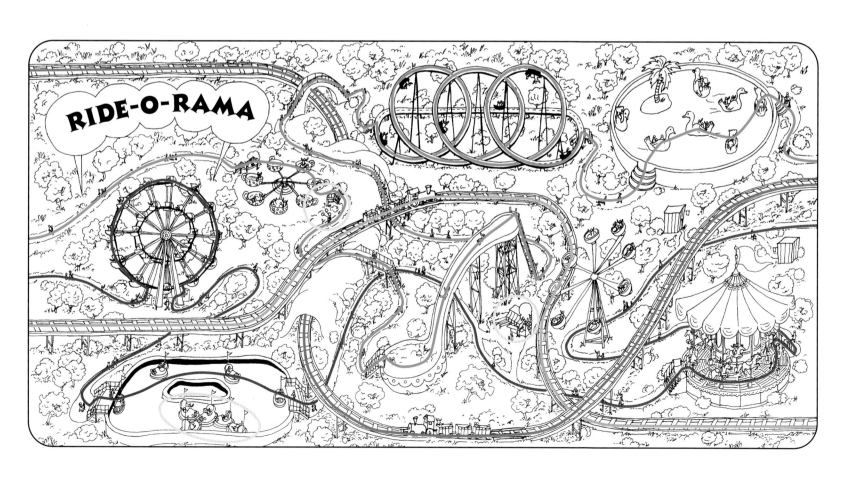

RIDE-O-RAMA

35

PIRATE'S COVE

MAGIC GARDEN

GET-LOST GRID

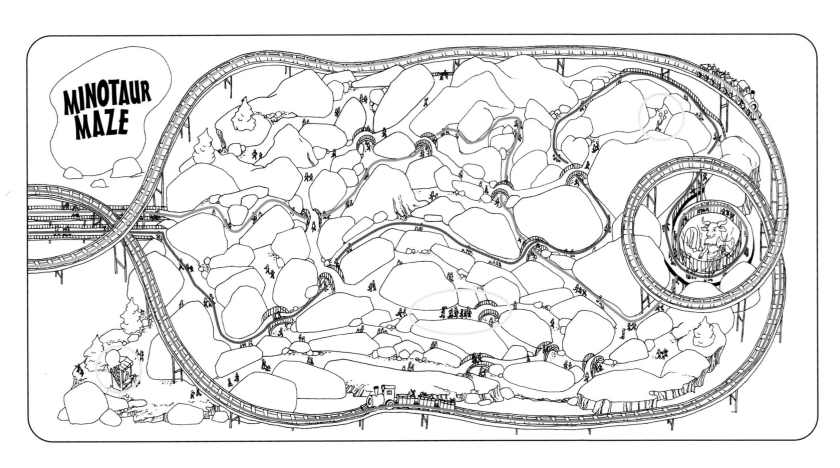

MINOTAUR MAZE